Poetic Celebration: The 20th Year

Olusheyi Banjo

Published by Olusheyi Banjo, 2024.

While every precaution has been taken in the preparation of this book, the publisher assumes no responsibility for errors or omissions, or for damages resulting from the use of the information contained herein.

POETIC CELEBRATION: THE 20TH YEAR

First edition. November 25, 2024.

Copyright © 2024 Olusheyi Banjo.

ISBN: 979-8227617156

Written by Olusheyi Banjo.

Poetic Celebration:
the 20th Year

OLUSHEYI BANJO

poems by
Olusheyi A. Banjo
2024

Copyright © 2024 Read or Green Books

Albuquerque, New Mexico

Cover Art by: Marissa Praa

All rights reserved. No portion of this publication may be reproduced or transmitted in any form without prior permission of **Olusheyi A. Banjo** unless such copying is expressly permitted by Federal copyright law. Addresses, questions, comments, send to: Read or Green Books: marissa@ReadorGreenBooks.com.

Visit our websites:

www.ReadorGreenBooks.com[1]

FIRST EDITION

Produced in the United States of America

---

1. http://www.readorgreenbooks.com

This book is dedicated to my beloved Uncle Olu and to my beloved Cousin Lisa Thompson, I know that you are in heaven, I hope to meet you both again someday.

Poetic Celebration:
the 20th Year

Foreword

This poetic collection is celebrating 20 years since my first published book "In Sorrow and Song" which was first published in 2005. I have come a very long way in my poetry and in my writing career since that day.

This is a celebration of how far I have come. In this poetry collection we have poems of celebration, poems of reflection, poems of silliness and even erotic poems. So, sit back and enjoy this poetic celebration with me.

Poetic Celebration

This is my poetic celebration
　　My wonderful jubilation
　　So glad that I'm still here
　　So glad that I survived
　　I thrived
　　Through the talk and such
　　I'm still around I thank God so much
　　So blessed
　　Beyond all mess
　　I passed the tests
　　Come celebrate with me
　　Celebrate being free
　　We made it we did it one more time
　　We got another chance to shine
　　So happy to celebrate 20 years of poetry
　　Of love of joy
　　Welcome to my poetic celebration

Soulmate

When I first met ya and we began to talk
    I got that strong feeling of love
    Love's walk
    We began to conversate more and more
    Every conversation made me know that it's you I adore
    With time I found out that we were meant to be
    You were meant to be just for me
    I found out that baby
    You're my soulmate
    my only love
    My sweet soulmate
    From up above
    The one that makes me complete
    You make being in love so sweet/
    Cause you're my only soulmate
    You make this half man feel like a whole
    You bring calming peace and sweetness to my soul
    You're my oasis in the storms of life
    You make even the darkness seem alright
    I prayed and God answered me
    He gave me this sweet lady
    We even think the same in my life
    I'm glad you came
    I have a wonderful lover and friend
    I'm so glad my broken heart you did mend
    Who could ask for anything more
    You opened my heart's door
    we're more than just lovers we are best friends
    I pray to God that our love never ends
    cause you are my true soulmate

We're so perfect for each other we even finish each others sentences
You are the right one
The only one
no one will replace your love
your face
I thank God he made you my soulmate

Know My Heart

No one else can see me like you do
    No one else knows when I'm being false or true
    No one else has the keys to my soul
    Has known me from day one
    Or even before day one
    You know my heart
    You feed my spirit
    Water my soul
    Lift me up when down in despair
    Heals my body and takes good care
    The only one who accepts and loves me unconditionally
    You love Olusheyi completely
    I do appreciate and love you
    That hear and answer my prayers
    Thank you God for always being there
    In my sorrow and my song
    In my melodies of silence
    In my joy
    Even in my ugliness of attitude
    So glad you know my heart and love me anyway

Basket Case

Man I am a basket case
    Just when I get over my ex and feeling fine.
    He calls me from jail
    I always accept and fall for his sweet talk.
    It's crazy that I am still such a basket for him

My Life's Philosphy

I play it cool and do the best that I can
    That's why I'm the man
    My philosophy of life is simple and the same
    Do good to others and play no games

Dreams

I still have dreams
    That have yet to be fulfilled
    I still have mountains
    That I have not climbed
    I want to write songs that the whole world to sing
    Not just to gain that bling bling
    Want to live good with my lover man
    Want to live the best I can
    Want to live my dream of being on a sitcom
    Making people laugh and calm
    I dream of doing these things and more
    Living life with happiness galore

Forever

Forever
> That's how long that I want this joy to last
> Forever
> Not in the past
> Forever
> With no time limit
> No time restraints
> No living in angst
> Forever
> And even one day
> Forever
> Never go away

Word Play 20 (Faith Evans Songs)

Ain't nobody gave me sunny days and a love like this that's why I love you

I'm never gonna let you go so come over

You used to love me all night long and had me burnin' up again and again

Soon as I get home you had me mesmerized in your paradise

It was incomparable kissing you

But now you gets no love because I deserve more than you

You gave me something to talk about and had me keep the faith

I'm truly nothing without you so rejoice with me and the who doesn't matter

Skip To It

Skip to it
    Just do it
    Til you can't no more
    Groove with it
    Move lift it
    Til sweat comes out your pores
    Live life it
    Get it right it
    Just embrace the beat
    Out your seat it
    Greet greet it
    Sing notes the song
    Skip to it
    Dove do it all day long

Still Be Here

So grateful to still be here
    So awesome to still use my gift
    Climbing mountains of creativity
    Happy as I can be
    To still be here

It's All Love

Doesn't matter what you do or who you claim to be
It's all love from me
Don't matter if you're the Queen of England or a homeless man on the street
It's all love and respect complete
As long as you show me respect
Expect
The same and more from me
Give you the upmost and make you free
I'll let you be you and let me be me
Truly happy
It's all good
It's all love
It's all alright with me
Forever be
I'm A lover not a hater
I'm a congratulator
So it's all love
It's all love
It's all love to me

Everybody

Everybody's done something
    Ain't nobody perfect
    We just got to move on
    Drive on
    Cause we can't change the past
    Gotta keep on to the future
    Whatever that may be
    Live your life happy
    Live your life free
    No use staying up
    Stressing bout it
    Letting it keep you up at night
    That ain't right
    Just know if God forgave you
    Please forgive yourself
    You have so much to be thankful for
    So much spiritual wealth
    You are awesome
    Fantastic too
    You are fantastically you
    So be the king that you are
    Be the superstar
    And know
    That you are equal to everybody

Blissful State

I'm in a blissful state
    Oh this feels so great
    Feels like heaven is mine
    Life is so kind
    God has surely blessed
    His love has caressed
    Wanna jump wanna shout
    Tell everyone what this joy is about
    Dancing in my heart
    From this excitement I will never part
    Thank you master for this state
    This wonderful
    This super
    This fantastic
    This excellent
    This joyous
    This absolute
    Blissful state of mind and of heart

Robby

Fine as aged wine
    Yet so humble and my awesome bro
    Inside and out you are beautiful
    A winner of every great prize
    An awesome spirit with great life
    Singer, model and even sex symbol too
    To be honest I wish I could find an excellent man like you
    You listen to me when I rant and rave
    About life and the crazy involvements I get into
    You are truly XL in your personality
    Thank you for being a real friend to me
    You are not just a dumb muscle head jock
    You are a wonderful spirit who has life on lock
    You are every woman and man's dream
    You get the money that Cream
    You deserve all of the adoration that you get
    For you are larger than life
    You are the awesome incredible fantastic excellent stupendous
    Robby XL
    My friend and my bro

Gotta Do

Do what you gotta do
    Do it right
    I said do what you gotta do and do it right
    Make sure that you are livin' tight
    Put the stride in your step and prance around
    Live your life up and never down
    Do what you gotta do
    Come correct
    Cause I said so hay

Prayer

I believe in God, I believe in prayer
    I believe that God will meet you there
    When you are on your knees
    He will your voice heed
    If you are sincere and true
    God will grant your petition to you
    All you have to do is believe and it will be so
    Don't let your faith go
    Sometimes it may take a minute days maybe years
    But your prayer will be heard that's so clear
    Pray without ceasing never give up
    And God will fill your cup
    The prayers of the righteous are powerful
    Never let your prayer life go slow
    Pray continuously
    Pray without giving up
    Pray
    Just pray
    And God will meet you there today

Big Girls Have Fun Too (You Ain't Got Nothin' On Me)

What can a skinny bitch do that I can't
    I can do it 20 times better
    Last longer get that cheddar
    I can swallow it whole
    Satisfy you better make you loose control
    With me you gotta do it right
    Hit the right spot all night
    With them skinny hoes they stop it hurts
    I say gimme more daddy while I cling to you shirts
    Give it to me daddy make you overtime
    With me you ain't gotta give me none of your dimes
    Just give me that good lovin'
    More than kissing and huggin'
    I'll make you feel like a real man
    When you working it
    You skinny bitches ain't got nothing On Me
    No you ain't got nothing on me
    I'm large pleasingly plump and lovely
    Got a soul food body
    You can tell that I'll do it right
    Why not try me tonight
    Give this big girl a chance
    I promise you'll be satisfied and you'll dance
    Cause big girls just do it better

I'm a Mess

I'm a mess
　　But I'm still blessed
　　Cause I win and pass life's tests
　　Still goin strong to this day
　　Heyyy
　　I'm ok
　　I can laugh at myself
　　Cause I got non material wealth
　　I can gladly say
　　I'm a mess.
　　But I am still blessed

You Were Never Mine

How can someone steal a lover that is yours
    It can't be done
    You were never mine to begin with
    We had a passing fling
    A passing thing
    Short time pleasure
    Beyond measure
    What we had was fun
    Real fun
    But it has to be over
    A 2 night stand
    You will never be my fuck buddy
    No you'll never be my dream man
    Even though you put it down
    You couldn't stay around
    While he said he took you away from me
    I just laughed and said I gladly gave you to him
    Hope he inherits your down Low drama
    The secret booty calls
    It's too bad that you don't love yourself
    Enough to be yourself
    I say goodbye and I hope you find your true self
    Instead of being so scared to be bisexual or even gay
    You were never mine
    So that's why I ain't sad or even crying

Zaddy

You're my zaddy
   My dream man come true
   You put it down in and out of the bedroom too
   You make me smile and feel so happy and true
   You know how to treat me in public
   You proudly hold my hand
   Yet you are a real man
   Your swag is amazing really heaven sent
   You are so priceless like the 1,000,000,000 mint
   Oh I love you zaddy, my king, my one
   You brighten my life like the sun
   My zaddy
   My wonderful sexy zaddy

Shoot Your Shot

Shoot your shot
    Why not
    Show me what you got
    Try to get me baby
    I promise I won't treat you shady
    If you come for real
    Tell me the real deal
    Don't overkill
    Gimme my fill
    I'll eat you like my last meal
    If you just shoot your shot
    Correctly

The Walk

Ryan took a walk with his wife Ashley.
They saw the beautiful city.
They saw beautiful shops
They saw a beautiful clothing company
They also saw ugly hole in the walls on the ugly street
They saw a homeless man dealing with hurt
They ended their walk more in love than ever before
It was a good walk

You're a Winner

You're a winner
    Not a beginner
    If you keep on standing strong
    You're a winner
    Not a sinner
    If you keep going on
    You're a winner
    Not a splinter
    If you keep running this life's crazy race
    You're a winner
    Not a sprinter
    If you hold on and keep up the right pace
    You're a winner
    not a sinner
    If you see it through
    You're a winner
    Not a monster
    If you just stay being wonderfully you

Center of Our Universe (Earth, Wind, Water, and Fire)

Earth
You are the creator of the earth
The sky
The seas
Plus everyone in it
A life giver
That made me out if dust
Wind
Let your mighty wind consume my soul
Your holy wind blow through me and make me whole
Let it blow the evil away
Make my life ok
Water
Your holy water washes my sins and sorrows away
Takes away the ills and pains of this life
Makes me alright
Lord you are the center of my being
The reason I live
The center of my universe
I cannot make it in this life without you guiding and leading me
What am I without you
Just dust
lower than the ground
Just ashes
that are easily blown away
A insignificant lump
A tree stump
A tear

that no one cries
A bed full of lies
An afterthought
Nothing
Nothing
Nothing
Am I
Without the center of my universe

I Wish

I wish this world was more accepting and loving
I wish there were no judgmental people
You could easily be happy and be yourself
I wish it was easy to find your soulmate
I wish every day could be sunny and bright
No rain no snow
Just beautifulness
I wish we still lived in Garden of Eden
We lived in paradise
I wish I was skinny and muscular
I wish I lived in a better area
I wish I made more money
Don't wanna be rich just comfortable
I wish I were straight instead of a man lover
I wish I could be honest and loved
Instead of hated because of who I love
It's not your business anyway
I wish I had a #1 on all of the charts
I wish I could win all of the awards
Grammy, Oscar, Emmy, Tony
Even NAACP
I wish someone important would notice me
I wish me and sister could live in peace
Be closer like a real brother and sister should be
Instead of her holding on to the past
I wish I could be more time conscience
I wish people couldn't tell that I am gay or sgl
I wish I wasn't so flirty
Or even extremely horny
I'm supposed to calm down with age

But
my hormones are still raging like a 20 year old's
I wish I could get with one of these fine firemen at my job
I wish I had the one
The man of my dreams
The one to cuddle up to
And to satisfy him
He will also satisfy me
With beautiful love
Not just in the bedroom
But in my whole life as well
All these things are in my mind all the time
All these wishes I would love to come true
Someday...may be soon

Joy

Something about the colors of the rainbow brings me joy
The reds, the blues, the purples, the greens the yellows
Even the lavender too
Seeing the rainbow in the sky reminds me of God's promise
God's never-ending love for humanity
That also brings me joy
To know that small me
Is loved by big him
I am worth loving
I am worth living
No matter my size
Or the size of my thighs
Or even my eyes
That's what I feel when I see the rainbow in the sky
Joyful
Joyous
Joy living
Positivity
That's me

Big Dick Willie

Big Dick Willie
    He's so silly
    He thinks the size of his dick makes him a man
    He thinks he's so grand
    He does everything that moves
    Yes he's that kind of dude
    That some women foolishly choose
    He should know that it's not the motion
    In the ocean
    Not the passion in the potion
    But the love that's in your heart
    And no other part
    That makes real love last

Aaliyah (20 years later)

You left us 2 decades ago
    But it seems like yesterday
    The one in a million baby
    moved to a heavenly realm
    Though we still miss you
    And we can't help but wonder what if
    We are at peace with the fact that you are at rest
    Flying high like an angel at your best
    We still jam to back and forth try again and are you that somebody
    We rejoice in the fact that you are no longer heartbroken
    You have found your resolution
    Up with our heavenly father
    We will forever love and miss you
    Our baby girl
    Our highest most exalted one
    Our princess of r&b
    Continue to rest in peace
    Aaliyah Dana Haughington

Lil AB

So young so full of life
    So full of light in this dark world
    So encouraging
    So full of zing
    Musically gifted
    Music was in your soul
    So sad to see you go
    You would always share music with me
    Encourage me
    I will miss you always asking
    When are we going to do some music together
    Now you're making heavenly music
    With all of the greats that have gone on before
    Your spirit has to soar
    Though we are left with so many questions
    Only the Heavenly father has the answer
    We will miss your physically
    We know that you're always here spiritually
    Be free Lil AB
    Rest in peace eternally

To Deadlee my Zaddy

You know what I want
    You know what I need
    Pull down your pants
    And gimme that seed
    You can give it to me while your smokin' weed
    Just give me that man juice
    I won't turn it loose
    Until you and I
    are satisfied
    This horniness I don't wanna hide
    I just wanna be your freak
    Zaddy
    Give it all to me
    I won't stop until you're drained
    Say my name
    Say my name
    Cum for me zaddy

Fabian Alomar

You're an awesome talented handsome Gemini brotha
    A skater, comedian, superstar like no othà
    The one that everyone wants to see
    Every man wants to be
    You came through so much like a real champ
    Been through the darkest hour, but now you're shining like a lamp
    And that is awesome to me
    You once we're a caged bird, but now you're flying free
    Showing the world again that you can't be stopped
    That your head will never again drop
    Never let the world make you feel that you're not all that because of
your past
    If they do put them on blast
    And tell them I am Fabian Alomar a winner through and through
    I am fantastic multi talented and better than you

Fresh Thoughts

What should I do
    Where should I go
    When I wanna find a love but all I find is hoes
    What's the plan
    Where can I find a good man
    Maybe I'll look in the haystack
    Maybe I'll go to a foreign country and never come back
    Maybe in England or Paris or even Madrid
    He'll probably be there and won't be hid
    Maybe in my fantasy
    Cause it sho ain't happening in my reality
    I don't know maybe I'm too obsessed
    Can't pass this love test
    Maybe I will one day

Hollywood Dick

You've got that Hollywood Dick
    Like a superstar everyone wants it
    Thick and juicy
    Made for this bussy
    A dick that will make anyone fiend
    Made for a hot sexy porno scene
    Forget all my lines just thinking about your cock
    Baby you rock
    You perform better than an actor, perform right on cue
    Michael B. Jordan ain't got nothing on you
    Give it to me better than any movie show
    You make me feel like I'm the best hoe
    In and out up and down
    I love it when you put it down
    Plus your cum tastes so sweet
    I love it when he you skeet
    Ooh daddy I love your Hollywood Dick

You Ain't Foolin' Me

You ain't foolin' me
    I know you get down, I know you're dirty
    For the right man,you'll get flirty
    I know that you have a type
    That you'll go gay for a gangsta, that's right
    You pretend you're hard and gangsta to the masses
    But I know in private you be giving up that asses
    You'll go down in a minute for the right man
    You'll pop your lips around his can
    You ain't foolin' me, I can see right through
    I look and I can tell you
    What you do
    How, cause I've been around
    Around them dl men for a long time in all towns
    You ain't foolin' me, you might as well come clean
    Cause bitch I know you love the peen

What Would the World Be Without Dreamers

What the world be without dreamers
    A cold and dreary place
    There would be no inventions
    No airplanes flying in the sky
    No cars on the road
    No cellphones
    No television sets
    No modern day inventions
    No love at all
    No creativity
    No humans to enjoy all of these things
    For God created the dreamers
    He gave the dreamers dreams to dream
    Created the beauty of dreams in everything
    So I say
    What would the world be without dreamers
    I think nothing at all

You Got My Heart

You got my heart and my soul
    Your love has taken control of me
    No one else has me under their spell
    Such a pleasure to be in love with you
    Such joy fills me through and through
    To know that someone like you loves me
    To know I love you too
    Dreams of love do come true in this dark and crazy world
    I feel like I am a champion
    I feel like a winner
    I feel that I can conquer anything
    We are invincible together
    What a beautiful blessing it is
    To know that
    I got your heart and you got my heart as well

Infact Intact

Infact Intact
 Not holding back
 Infact Intact
 Stepping forward and never back
 Infact Intact
 What a wonderful thing
 Infact Intact
 My heart does sing
 Infact Intact
 To realize after all I've been through I'm still here
 Infact Intact
 This is a wonderful celebration of my wonderful life
 To know that I'm
 Infact still intact

Heart Racing

Every time I get a response from you
    My heart starts racing
    Every time you like a post on any of my social media
    I get so happy
    I'm crushing on you real hard
    You made me let down my guard
    Please don't be like the countless losers that I've liked and I've dated
    Please be the one that I'm supposed to be mated
    Please be the one
    I hope so
    Because
    Every time I see you, you send my heart racing

Goodbye Betty, Sidney, Bob, James, Andre, Meatloaf, Gilbert, and Louie

You made this crazy world a better place with your talent

A little bit brighter with your comedy music, comedy and joyfulness

Thank you for being our friends

Thank you for coming to dinner on an uptown Saturday night

Thank you for being a funny dad to my generation

Thank you for making us dance with juicy fruit and love with you me and he

Because of you we didn't have to do anything for love

Thank you for making the world a little bit more stylish

Life with you Louie was oh so sweet and funny too

You're delighting God, Jesus, the Holy Spirit and the angels too with your awesome talent

Though we must say Goodbye for now in the physical world

We know that you are forever near us with your spirit

Rest on you wonderful people, you have gained your wings for making this physical world a better place

Untitled

Sometimes I get lost
Lost in my thoughts
Lost in the abyss
Am I good enough
Am I a wannabe
Will I ever achieve the success that I want
Where am I going
What does the future hold for me
Will I be a successful preacher
Does my life really matter
Is anyone really listening to me when I try to motivate them
Am I just passing in the wind
Will I ever find the love that I seek
What's going on
Is my living in vain
Those are just some of the questions that fill my mind

Lord

Lord I just want to do what you would have me to do
    For as long as you want me to do it
    Though this world is such a mess
    Sometimes life can take you through crazy tests
    I just want to stay in your will for my life
    Follow your ultimate plan
    I'm not happy unless I'm living in your purpose for my life
    Sin is pleasurable and fun for awhile
    But in the end it can make you frown and not smile
    My prayer is that I be a man of you and not of myself
    Help me to sacrifice self will
    Help me sacrifice wanting to please the people of the world
    Cause if you're not pleased, what's the use
    Why do it if it's not giving you glory
    Lord I want to please you wholeheartedly
    That's the only way my spirit can be free and happy

Forgive Yourself

Learn to forgive yourself for your past
    The past doesn't last
    Learn to move on with your life
    I know your past may be painful
    Or downright shameful
    But somehow some way you have to move on
    You have to be strong
    If you're stuck in the past, you can't move to a bright future
    You can't accept the gift that is the present
    Protect your essence
    Nothing that you've done is worth constantly torturing yourself over
    Find your four leaf clover
    And simply forgive yourself

Your Love

Your Love has made me a better man
    A better human
    I can call this half man whole
    I can tell the world that it's because you made me so
    I am a stronger man who has a tender side
    Because of you
    My lovely loving boo
    I truly thank you
    For you unconditional real love
    That has changed my hard cold heart
    I used to be a player
    A real slut, but your love changed all that
    Every day I wake up I say
    Thank you God for your real love
    Your Love is so golden to me
    Because it has set this prisoner free

I Secretly Love You

Can't tell nobody about what I feel
    But I know that it is real
    Don't wanna be a stalker
    Nor a hawker
    But I can't deny my feeling
    I dream of you at night
    In my dreams it feels so right
    You were meant for me and I was meant for you
    That's the way it should be
    Or at least how it is in my fantasy
    I don't know why but I secretly love you

Ain't Nothin' but God

Who is my healer when I'm on my sickbed
    Ain't nothin' but God
    Who is my friend when no one is around
    Ain't nothin' but God
    Who is my protector when danger surrounds
    Ain't nothin but God
    Who gives me love and victory every day
    Ain't nothin but God
    Who is with me every step of the way
    Ain't nothin' but God
    Who gives me a wonderful song to sing
    Ain't nothin' but God
    Who is my king of Kings
    Ain't nothin but God
    Who is the reason that I am still here breathin' today
    Ain't nothin but God
    Who wipes all my tears away
    Ain't nothin but God
    There is no one who can even compare
    He knows me and he cares
    He is aware
    He is always there
    I tried the rest but all I can say is
    Ain't no one
    Ain't nobody like
    Ain't nothin but God

Frickin Beautiful (to B0ryan)

Gotta give props and glory to God for making you
    And I wanna thank your momma and daddy too
    Like the statue of David, you are a wonderful work of art
    I love you every part
    Your beauty is unbelievable
    I don't want to stop looking at you
    Gets me excited, my pulse starts to race
    At the sight of your lovely face
    Your personality is also from heaven above
    Good God it I love
    You can carry on a conversation
    Sweet sensation
    I can be in your presence for hours and not get tired at all.
    You are big and tall
    My Lord you are Frickin beautiful

Fuck Me

I've been wanting you since the first time I saw you
I 've been wanting you to fuck me
Make me scream your name
Let me lick your big delicious lollipop
Give me the treat you know I deserve
I'm excited just thinking about you
I'll make you excited too
Give me your best
I'll give you mine
There is nothing like the passion that we elude
Kiss me while you're in me
Talk dirty to me
Yes, I'm your nasty faggot bitch
I'm precuming thinking about you
Oh please Daddy Papi lover
Fuck me

Another Couch Potatoes Nightmare

My fire stick is stuck
    Stuck in bad new show land
    Instead of reality shows, bad news is all that's being shown
    A flood here, food shortage, even mass murderers
    When will it stop when will it end
    I need to watch a comedy maybe
    But the new ones aren't funny
    They are pathetic and disrespectful
    Maybe a superhero movie
    But they aren't cool either
    They just fly around and try to be political
    Maybe I need a cartoon
    But they use more fowlness
    Is this cartoon for kids or adults
    I don't know
    None of these channels are good
    Tubi, Fox+, ABCplus even Disney plus too
    I'm going to turn off my fire stick and go read a book

Vanilla in my Chocolate

I like a little vanilla in my chocolate every now and then
    A little cream in my coffee
    A little marshmallow in my cocoa
    That just makes my senses go
    Give it to me
    I need it now
    Someway somehow
    Just give the lovely white candy to your baby
    Make it sweet and gooey
    Tutti fruity
    I'll be your raw booty
    Your milk chocolate treat
    Your black licorice sweet
    Put your vanilla in this chocolate

Unofficially My Man

I claim you to all of my friends
I brag about you all the time
I tell everyone that I meet
That your love is so sweet
Even though we're not exclusive
My heart has your heart and no can be intrusive
Even though we never said it publicly
We're keeping our privacy
You're still mine and I am yours
I want to shout it out loud on Mount Everest
That you are the best
Thing that's ever happened to me
You feel me with glee
I love you with my heart mind and soul
No other has control
Of me
Ooh baby
I hate it that you're unofficially my man

Magic

That magic lives in me
    The magic that sets a heart free
    That magic that can bring a smile to a dark face
    That magic that is wonderful like saving grace
    That magic that can strut and make others strut along
    That magic that can create a meaningful poem, play or song
    That magic that encourages
    That magic that flourishes
    But why do I keep giving that magic to folks that don't appreciate
    That hate
    I'm going to stop that mess
    Start living blessed
    And live in my magical purpose

You Can't Buy the World

You can't buy the world, it would cost too much

You can't supersede God, he's too powerful

You can't escape reality, it will find you wherever you try to hide

You can't be the most absolute perfect person in the world, it's just not possible

Just live the best you can be

Live in your means

And learn to be happy with what you have

Lover

I'm your lover man
    I'm here for you baby
    You've been hurt so bad
    You feel crazy
    You feel so sad
    You don't even wanna trust again
    Where's your love
    Where's your friend
    You know what
    I've come to show you that
    I'm here for you
    I'm here to give you love
    Love that is divine
    Love that is so true
    I'm your lover man
    I'm your lover
    Trust in me baby
    Cause I'm your lover man
    I'm your lover
    Your lover man
    I'm your lover
    Put your heart in my hands
    I'm your lover
    Your lover man
    Trust in me
    You will see that I'm lover
    Your lover man
    I'll make everyday Valentine's Day
    I'll give you roses flowers candy
    Anything that you want

I'll do it all/for you
I'll make you feel like your a queen
Royalty
You'll never have to look for nobody
Nobody but me
I'm here to show you unconditional agape love
That's what you need
You don't need anyone else
You don't need to cry no more
Let me your Valentine
Let me be your lover
Your one and only
Lover man

Livin' For Love

I'm just living for love y'all
    Every day I wake up
    I'm asking
    what can I do to make this world a better place
    Who can I make happy
    Who can I love today
    Who can I just bring joy to today
    I'm living for love
    I wish everybody was living for love
    This world will be a better place
    I'm living for love
    I'm just living the dream
    I'm just living for love
    and
    I'm giving all of my love
    Every day I'm thinking of who can I make smile today
    Who can I give love to today
    Who can I cheer up
    Who can I be an inspiration to
    Who can I makes life a better place
    Who can I just give a loving smile to
    Who can I make feel better who is down
    That's what I'm living for
    We all need to be like that y'all
    Bring some love y'all
    I was born to be a lover
    I was born to be somebody who encourages people
    I was born to just love you
    I know sometimes this world is just so full of hate
    But I'm here to bring some love to you

I'm living to make you happy
I'm living to make you smile
I'm living to bring dt joy to your life
When you don't have it
That's why I'm here
If you need some love
All you have to do is call on me
Cause that's what I'm living for
I'm living for love
You know love is a free gift
Embrace the gift
Embrace the love
That's why I'm living
Everyone needs to be encouraging to everyone
That's what it's all about
That's why we're living
That's why I'm living
I'm living for love
Are you living for love

Return to the Love Room

It's time to return to the love room
> We've been gone for too long
> it's time to return to the love room baby
> Let's go back to the love room
> Let's return to love
> let's go back to the love room with the feeling from above
> Brothers and sisters/it's time to return to love
> Return to embracing each other
> Return to our understanding
> It's time for us to return to feeling so good about each other
> It's time for us to just love each other
> Let's return to togetherness
> Brothers and sisters
> We've been fighting each other for too long
> We've been starting wars that we really don't need
> It's time for us to love again
> It's time for us to feel good again
> It's time for us to be one family under God
> Indivisible
> Let's bring some love
> Bring some unity
> Let's bring some love
> Let's bring some unity
> Hug your brother
> Hug your sister
> We are all that we have in this world
> If we don't love it's gonna be over
> Let's bring some love

If I Was Born a White Girl

If I was born a white girl
    These crazy niggas would love me so
    They would bend over backwards to do things for me
    They would call me sexy
    Do anything to be around me
    They would call me beauty
    They would make me their queen
    They would even turn their backs on their own race for me
    They would cuss out their sistas just to get a taste of my sweet vaginal
nectar
    I could call them out their name
    And make them feel ashamed
    To be their race
    Make them ashamed of their black face
    Life would be so much easier for me
    If I were a beautiful white girl

Hated Because Of My Skin Color

America is sick, sick with an incurable disease
    This disease is as old as the Constitution or the Bill of Rights
    It still isn't right
    This disease is running rampant throughout this land
    This disease has destroyed many innocent lives
    Cause many innocent people to die
    This disease is making folks turn against each other
    Who kill their sisters and brothers of another color
    The disease of racism, the disease of haterism
    What is the solution, what is the cure
    When will it be cured
    The answer is unknown

I understand

I understand that you're hurting
    I understand your pain
    But you don't have to try to make me miserable like you
    I thought I was your boy
    Your homie true
    But yet you're trying to make me miserable and that ain't cool
    Can't share nothing good with you
    Because you'll try to bring me down and make me cry
    But no matter what you say or do
    I'll still be awesome
    And I understand that you feel inferior

20 Years later

20 years later and I'm still speaking from my heart
    Still coming with the real
    Writing poems that you can feel
    You get your love on too
    That can make you feel cool to
    Poems that you can say to your lover
    Or any other
    Poems of triumph and tragedy
    Poems of madness of gladness for you and me
    20 years later and I'm still going strong
    Wanna be doing this for another 20 years

Time Goes By

Time goes by rather quickly, especially as you get older
    Seems like the days get shorter and shorter
    The nights just zoom right on by
    The weeks seems like a day
    The seasons like an endless week
    The weekend seems like mere hours
    A sunrise like a glimpse
    A moon light like a spec
    As I get older I learned to respect time
    I learn to never waste time
    To keep moving until my clock runs out
    For we never know the time or the season
    Seems like just yesterday I was in my teens and my twenties
    Then marched on to my thirties
    Now I'm in my 40's
    All I can say is
    My goodness how the time goes by

Fickle Jickle 3

Fickle Jickle lost his sickle
    And he can't find it
    Looking in bed or in his living room
    Looked in his kitchen or the refrigerator behind the mushrooms
    He looked in his car
    But that didn't get him far
    He looked at his job
    But that made him sob
    He looked and finally found it
    Yes he found it
    Where
    Not here
    Not there
    He found it in a pair
    Of his pants

Happy Pride (I am Proud)

For years I used to let others tell me
    That there was something wrong with me
    That I had to be a certain way to be happy
    That hell is my home if I don't conform
    I wasn't in the norm
    But now I realize
    Ain't nothing wrong with me
    I have so much to be proud of
    I am truly proud to be me
    I am a son, a father, a grandfather and a proud gay man
    I am truly awesome
    I walk down the street with my head held high
    Beaming with pride
    I am proud
    Yes I am so proud
    Really proud to just be Olusheyi

Need You

With you all my mountains are easier to climb
  With you my valleys aren't that low
  With you I feel like superman/I can conquer anything
  Because You are everything
  Plus so much more
  Baby it's you I adore
  I need you all the pain you take away
  Not the same when you're with me
  I need you
  those grey clouds just fade away
  and everything feels better babe
  With you

Vacation Texas Style

Feels so good to be on this vacation
    Getting away
    From the stress of LA
    Seeing my friends
    Connecting to family
    Just letting the good times roll, letting it be
    Getting my relaxation on
    Feeling rested and strong
    Even getting some good lovin' too
    That's stress relief, so awesome and cool
    This Texas vacation is Wonderful
    I wish this could last awhile
    But I gotta get back to my life
    The hustle, the bustle, the strife
    I'm not worried about that today
    I'm just going to enjoy my day
    Today

It's Alright

It's alright if you ignore me
    It's alright if you try to put me down
    It's alright if you disown me
    Won't repost my birthday tributes at all
    Try to make me feel low as the ground
    Cause I'm rising up, no coming down in sight
    I'm living it up, living the good life
    I am a super duper star
    My gifts are taking me so far
    I'm out of the stratosphere
    While you're stuck down here
    Life is making me a winner
    Never a beginner
    Too tight
    Too tight
    Treat me bad if you want to
    It's alright

Only One God

There is only one God
Yet he has many names
Creator of the universe, Yahweh Eloheim, Jehova, Allah
King of Kings, Everlasting father, all that we need
Most High
Even in the not so good times we should give him honor
Give him his props
He deserves it
Who else is almighty
Who else is infinite
There since the beginning
Will be here in the end
He's in control of all things
The great and the small
Everywhere at the same time
No one else can do that
So big yet he cares about the small
The little ones
What else can I say
But
There is only one God but he has so many names

Anthony Gray (My King)

Everything about you is regal
> Everything about you is grand
> You are a king, a king of a man
> Your presence demands respect and admiration
> At the very sight of you commands jubilation
> Very intelligent and deep too
> I love just talking to you
> High above the ordinary
> Almost extraordinary
> Are your actions and speech
> Oh king I beseech
> You please stay in my life
> Cause you make my life alright
> I love that I can talk to you and you understand
> You are more just the man
> You are it
> The shit
> There's nothing more I can say but
> You are so awesome
> An awesome King to me

One of Us

You're one of us
> Really one of us
> Part of our family
> Welcome to our poetic and artistic family
> Where we share our stories
> Our loves
> Our lives
> Even our hates
> Where we write and express
> To impress
> Nor repress
> Just be blessed
> We give encouragement to just be yourself
> No one else
> We are all colors of the rainbow
> All sexual preferences
> All nationalities
> We are free
> We may not be blood but we have a beautiful bond
> A bond based on our love of art
> And every other part
> So we happily say
> You're one of us
> Our poetry writing
> Living
> And artistic family

Real Talk

I can remember a time
    A time when I told the world about me
    Some were cool
    Some were cruel
    My mom said I had a boy not a girl
    I felt crushed, but somehow I survived
    But with time I learned to accept me
    I am not going to hell,
    I am not a mental health failure
    I am not a deviant
    I am out, I am proud
    Say it loud
    I am LGBT
    SGL
    Queer
    Wonderful
    I'm Embracing your rainbow
    I have nothing to be ashamed of
    Awesome am I
    I am fly
    and I live with pride

Prayer

I believe in God, I believe in prayer
    I believe that God will meet you there
    When you are on your knees
    He will your voice heed
    If you are sincere and true
    God will grant your petition to you
    All you have to do is believe and it will be so
    Don't let your faith go
    Sometimes it may take a minute days maybe years
    But your prayer will be heard that's so clear
    Pray without ceasing never give up
    And God will fill your cup
    The prayers 9f the righteous are powerful
    Never let your prayer life go slow
    Pray continuously
    Pray without giving up
    Pray
    Just pray
    And God will meet you there today

To Joseph A.

When the clouds gather and drown out your sun
    Remember to keep smiling and still have fun
    When you feel like crying and sadness is near
    Don't give up your friend Olu is here
    When no words will come out and you're voice is gone
    Please my friend stay strong
    When you feel in defeat
    And you can't move your feet
    Just call me and you I'll greet
    Cause we all need a friend whose burdens of life that we can share
    We all need some love and to know someone cares
    I got you cause I know you got me
    I'm your friend really
    You'll never be alone my friend
    Cause I'm here in spirit and whenever you need
    I'm your friend no matter what

Double Dose of Joy

You came 13 days early and brought me a double dose of joy
    Just when I needed it
    You brought even more sunshine into my life
    I'm smiling, filled with joy, skipping and even dancing
    There's nothing like seeing a new life beginning.
    Your legacy going on
    Going on strong
    Nothing can or will bring down this grandpa, because of his boys
    My two new sunshines
    The happiness of my heart
    This joy is so wonderful that I don't want it to end
    Can't believe that I have grandsons that are twins
    David and Soloman, what wonderful names
    May your future be bright
    May you go to the highest heights of life
    May your life be filled with joy and no strife
    May you both be great men, the best that you can be
    You are destined to be great because you are apart of me
    Pop pop loves you both more than you know
    I can't wait to see you grow
    You both are my double dose of Joy

Beautiful Africa

Oh beautiful mother Africa
    How beautiful you are
    Oh beautiful mother Africa
    The most beautiful of them all
    Oh iya lẹwa Africa
    Bawo ni o ṣe lẹwa
    Oh iya lẹwa Africa
    Julọ lẹwa ti gbogbo wọn
    Oh muhle mama Africa
    Umuhle kanjani
    Oh muhle mama Africa
    Enhle kunabo bonke
    Oh muhle mama Africa
    Umuhle kanjani
    Oh muhle mama Africa
    Enhle kunabo wote
    ◇◇ ◇◇◇◇◇ ◇◇ ◇◇◇◇◇◇◇
    ◇◇◇◇ ◇◇ ◇◇◇◇◇◇
    ◇◇ ◇◇◇◇◇◇ ◇◇ ◇◇◇◇◇◇◇
    ◇◇◇◇◇ ◇◇◇◇ ◇◇◇◇◇ ◇◇◇◇◇◇ ◇◇◇◇◇◇
    Oh belle mère Afrique
    Comme tu es belle
    Oh belle mère Afrique
    Le plus beau de tous
    Ag pragtige moeder Afrika
    Hoe mooi jy is
    Ag pragtige moeder Afrika
    Die mooiste van hulle almal
    Yewe mama mwiza Afrika
    Mbega ubwiza

Yewe mama mwiza Afrika

Ubwiza muri bose

يا أم أفريقيا الجميلة

كم أنت جميل

يا أم أفريقيا الجميلة

أجملهم جميعا

Oh bèl manman Afrik

Ala bèl ou bèl

Oh bèl manman Afrik

Pi bèl nan yo tout

Oh bèl manman Африка

Ала бел или бел

Oh bèl manman Африка

Pi bèl nan yo tout

Life Be Lifein

Life just be Lifein
    Sometimes the good turns to triflin
    Sometimes the sun turns to rain
    The happiness turns to pain
    Smiles turns to frowns
    The ups turns to downs
    Sometimes the still turns to earthquakes
    That makes your very faith shake
    Answers turns to questions
    But through it all, it's all lessons
    And a blessing
    That's why I don't worry when
    Life Be Lifein

Get To Know You

You call me a fool
Because I don't wanna be taken care of by you
I just want to get to know you
Don't matter how much money
That you try to throw at me,
Real love comes for free
Your checkbook
Won't get me hooked
Gotta have personality
Gotta make my heart sing
Not just be a one night thing
Or just a fling
You're used to buying people
But I'm not for sale
I don't want to go through hell
All I want is your love
Your real love
For us to have romantic walks on the beach
Or swim together in shallow creek
To go out to movies and dinner too
For you to really love me and I really love you
Some may call me a fool
But I will say this plain and true
Fuck your money, all I want is to get to know you

One More For The Reader 20

We celebrated, we reflected we even laughed too
    We reflected, We sang and we even got angry
    It was a dynamic 20th year celebration
    Celebration of poetry and music
    I can't believe that we made it this far
    To our 20th year
    We made it through the storm
    Through the criticism
    So glad that you're on this journey with me
    Let us keep celebrating until we meet again
    Stay wonderful stay awesome until we take another poetice journey
together

Acknowledgements

I want to say thank you to everyone who has been there for me and has been rocking with me for these last 20 years. God, thank you for giving me this talent. I promise that I will use it to bring you glory.

Thank you to my awesome family from around the world, Momma, my big brother Olusegune, My big sister Olubunmi, My wonderful Daughter Kaniah, my son in law Deshawn, My wonderful grandchildren, Carla Patricia, DJ, Issac, Shayla June, David and Soloman. To my aunts, uncles, cousins and other family from around the world I love you.

Thank you to my awesome House of Refuge Church of God in Christ Church family. I appreciate every one of you. To Deon Joseph and the Downtown Clergy council you all are the best. To my wonderful friends, Donnie, Tom, Robert Forman, Anthony Desire, Anthony Gray, Young Sun, I thank you for holding me up.

Special thank you to my friend and producer Carl Anthony, thank you for being there for me and producing the great music.

Thank you to my boy, my video directing homie, Nitro Geez, my dawg for life, love you bro. To my poetic family (Nick, Andrew, Midnight, Dee Allen, Nikki, Caesar, jessy) from around the world, you are my inspiration. I love you forever Robert Jackson (Robby XL.) You truly are XL to me. To my Faith International Seminary family, I love all of you.

Also Thank you to my Big O's Top 20 Countdown family as well, I sincerely appreciate you. To anyone that I forgot to name, charge it to my head and not my heart.

About the Author

Olusheyi (pronounced "o-loo-shay-e") Banjo aka Pastor O, His first single 'Keep Hope Alive' was released in 2002. In 2005 his first poetry book "In Sorrow and Song" was published. He has published 21 other books including his first children's book and his autobiography "I Ain't Ashamed: The Life Adventures Of Minister Olusheyi Banjo." His first full length gospel album "Look What God Has Done" was released in 2006,followed by 24 more musical projects. He won the Akademia's Best Christian Hip-Hop album award in March 2015. He also has been nominated for six Southern California Gospel Music Awards. In 2013,Olusheyi graduated from Bethany Christian Bible College with his degree in Theology. He made his on stage debut in a play titled "Come As You Are" in 2009 followed by his first non church play titled "Love On San Pedro" in 2013. Since then he has appeared in 9 other stage productions. Olusheyi was ordained as a minister on September 23,2013. He is also a comedian, who has been performing on stage since 2010. He is host of Big O's Top 20 Countdown since 2016. His 20th album 4020 was released June 3rd 2020. His 21rst album Welcome To The Love Room was released February 14,2021 and featured the title track which became his biggest single to date. He has also won 2 X-Poze-ing Music Awards for album of the year for 4020 and Best R&B single for "Joyful Return." His second children's book titled Lacy Gracie And Tawn Learn About Bullying was released on November 21,2022. His 190th single "Livin' For Love" was released On January 1,2024 and gained 100,000 plus views on Youtube within 2 days of its release. His 25th album "Return To The Love Room" was released on February 14,2024. His 200th single Dream Of Love was released June 28,2024.

About the Author

Olusheyi is an awesome person Olusheyi is a goal oriented person who has a lot of love and loves to be good to people. He is a singer, songwriter,journalist, comedian,bible scholar,author, actor and entrepreneur. He has 3 gospel Cds that has been released (1.Look What God Has Done (Oct.10,2006) 2.Olusheyi(originally released on Nov. 17, 2009,re-released on May 24, 2011) 3.Joyful Return (Dec. 10,2010) He released his first single "Keep Hope Alive" on March 30,2002. Olusheyi has authored 2 poetry books 1."In Sorrow And Song"(March 10,2005) and 2."Hitchhiking Down Life's Highway" (March 25,2010.) He is working on 5 projects (a Children's book, 3rd and 4th poetry books. "Choose The Stars,""Galatic Underground," a book of reflections & his 4th CD "Growing In Faith") All scheduled to be released in 2012. Stay tuned

www.ingramcontent.com/pod-product-compliance
Lightning Source LLC
Chambersburg PA
CBHW022035150726
47990CB00002B/972